W9-AFW-211

CHILDREN'S FAVORITE ACTIVITY SONGS

I'm a Little Teapot

Published in the United States of America by The Child's World®
1980 Lookout Drive • Mankato, MN 56003-1705
800-599-READ • www.childsworld.com

First published by Mathew Price Ltd.
5013 Golden Circle
Denton, TX 76208, USA.
Illustrations © 1987 Moira Kemp
Text © 1939 Kelman Music

Acknowledgments
The Child's World®: Mary Berendes, Publishing Director
Editorial Directions: E. Russell Primm, Editor; Lucia Raatma, Proofreader
The Design Lab: Kathleen Petelinsek, Art Direction and Design;
   Anna Petelinsek and Victoria Stanley, Page Production

Library of Congress Cataloging-in-Publication Data
I'm a little teapot / illustrated by Moira Kemp.
    p. cm. — (Children's favorite activity songs)
  ISBN 978-1-60253-192-5 (library bound : alk. paper)
  1. Finger play. 2. Nursery rhymes. I. Kemp, Moira, ill. II. Title.
  GV1218.F5I5 2009
  793.4—dc22   2009001565

ILLUSTRATED BY MOIRA KEMP

I'm a little teapot,
short and stout.

Here is my handle.

Here is my spout.

When I get all
steamed up,
hear me shout,

"Tip me over and pour me out!"

12

13

SONG ACTIVITY

Push your tummy out to make yourself round when you say:
I'm a little teapot, short and stout.

Place your hand on your hip for a handle:
Here is my handle.

Bend your other arm and hand like a spout:
Here is my spout.

Hold your breath and puff out your cheeks:
When I get all steamed up, hear me shout,

Bend over as if pouring from your spout:
"Tip me over and pour me out!"

BENEFITS OF NURSERY RHYMES AND ACTIVITY SONGS

Activity songs and nursery rhymes are more than just a fun way to pass the time. They are a rich source of intellectual, emotional, and physical development for a young child. Here are some of their benefits:

- Learning the words and activities builds the child's self-confidence—"I can do it all by myself!"

- The repetitious movements build coordination and motor skills.

- The close physical interaction between adult and child reinforces both physical and emotional bonding.

- In a context of "fun," the child learns the art of listening in order to learn.

- Learning the words expands the child's vocabulary. He or she learns the names of objects and actions that are both familiar and new.

- Repeating the words helps develop the child's memory.

- Learning the words is an important step toward learning to read.

- Reciting the words gives the child a grasp of English grammar and how it works. This enhances the development of language skills.

- The rhythms and rhyming patterns sharpen listening skills and teach the child how poetry works. Eventually the child learns to put together his or her own simple rhyming words— "I made a poem!"

ABOUT THE ILLUSTRATOR

Moira Kemp has illustrated dozens of books for children, including many Mother Goose rhymes and activity songs. Kemp studied history at Oxford University in England, but she soon discovered a love for children's books and illustrations. She studied at the Camberwell School of Arts and Crafts. Her books have sold more than 5 million copies. She lives in Middlesex, England.